DATE DUE

21st
Century
Skills Library

COOL CAREERS
MOVIE DIRECTOR

JOSEPH R. O'NEILL

Published in the United States of America by
Cherry Lake Publishing, Ann Arbor, Michigan
www.cherrylakepublishing.com

Content Adviser
Tom Dowd, Professor, Columbia College Chicago

Credits
Photos: Cover and page 1, ©Telepix/Alamy; page 4, ©Megapress/Alamy; page 6,
©Photogenix/Alamy; page 9, ©AP Photo/Cheboygan Daily Tribune, Shawna McManu;
page 10, ©Martin Thomas Photography/Alamy; page 12, ©Matt Cardy/Alamy;
page 14, ©Sipa via AP Images; page 16, ©Pictorial Press Ltd/Alamy; page 19,
©AP Photo/Tina Fineberg; page 20, ©Steve Skjold/Alamy; page 23, ©UK Stock
Images Ltd/Alamy; page 25, ©Susoy/Dreamstime.com; page 27, ©Pictorial Press
Ltd/Alamy; page 28, ©Kim Karpeles/Alamy

Library of Congress Cataloging-in-Publication Data
O'Neill, Joseph, 1979–
  Movie director / by Joseph O'Neill.
     p. cm.—(Cool careers)
  Includes index.
  ISBN-13: 978-1-60279-499-3
  ISBN-10: 1-60279-499-5
  1. Motion pictures—Production and direction—Juvenile literature.
I. Title. II. Series.
  PN1995.9.P7054 2009
  791.4302'33—dc22   2008050641

Cherry Lake Publishing would like to acknowledge
the work of The Partnership for 21st Century Skills.
Please visit *www.21stcenturyskills.org* for more information.

MOVIE DIRECTOR

TABLE OF CONTENTS

CHAPTER ONE

HOW MOVIES ARE MADE

When you go to the movies or watch a DVD at home, you are enjoying a complete and polished product. That product is the result of the efforts of many artists, technicians,

A lot goes on while filming a movie. Directors need good organizational skills to keep things running smoothly.

and crew members. Who oversees the many people involved in the moviemaking process? That is the job of the movie director.

Making a motion picture involves many stages. First, someone invents the characters and writes the **screenplay**. The producers of the movie use the screenplay to figure out how much the movie will cost. Then they hire the director. This person is in charge of making the movie. She hires actors. She works with the **cinematographer** to decide how the film should be shot. She also guides the actors in performing the movie's scenes. After the film is shot, the director works with **editors**. They piece together the scenes and check for mistakes.

The main job of the movie director is to imagine, shape, and guide the creation of the movie. The director must imagine the entire film before she can do any filming. She envisions how the film will look and sets the overall mood. This requires deciding things such as whether there will be many close-up shots or more wide views.

One of the first things a movie director must do is "block" the scenes of the movie. The director decides how the audience will see the movie's action unfold. To do this, she divides the action into shots that are filmed from different angles. You've probably noticed that a movie does not show all the action from only one point of view. Instead, the picture on the screen changes. The **perspective** of the viewer might follow first one character and then another. Some shots will be close-up. Other times, the shots will be from farther away. Even in a short scene, each of the shots must be planned in advance by the movie director.

The director also works with the rest of the crew to develop a shooting schedule. This schedule must be one that the entire **cast** and crew can follow. The schedule

Many scenes for the film **Casanova** *were shot in Italy. It can be expensive to film in foreign countries.*

LIFE & CAREER SKILLS

The director and producer must stick to a **budget**. This is very important. Movies are expensive to make. *The Dark Knight* (2008), for example, cost nearly $185 million to make. Costs include filming equipment, travel expenses, and cast and crew salaries.

Staying within budget often requires directors to be flexible. Unexpected problems are common on film sets. Maybe a certain scene will be too expensive to shoot. Will a different location lower costs? Should the scene be removed altogether? Directors must make these decisions quickly. Finishing a film within budget—and on time— depends on it.

determines the times and locations for filming each scene. Scenes are not filmed in the same order that they appear in the finished movie. Instead, each scene is filmed in an order that is convenient to the director and the production schedule. Do scenes at the beginning and end of the movie take place in the desert? Then the director will shoot those scenes together during one or two days of on-location filming. The rest of the movie might be shot in a studio or other locations around the world. The schedule also lets everyone know when the movie will be finished and ready for release. Careful scheduling allows a moviemaking team to work well together.

Selecting the actors who will appear in the film is one of the most important parts of the director's job. In most cases, **auditions** are held. During an audition, actors read lines from the screenplay in front of the director and her staff. This is a chance for the director to evaluate an actor and determine if that person is right for the part.

LEARNING & INNOVATION SKILLS

Movie directors must be able to communicate clearly with others. Actors, technicians, and others involved in making a film look to the director for leadership. The director must be able to tell them exactly what he wants them to do. If he doesn't communicate clearly, he runs the risk of the film not turning out the way he imagines it.

Auditions can be stressful. Actors work hard to get the lines just right and, hopefully, get the part.

CHAPTER TWO
LIGHTS, CAMERA, ACTION!

What exactly do movie directors do? Let's imagine a young director named Madison. She has just been contacted by Jay, a writer with a new screenplay called *The Mystery of the Magic Mansion*. It's about a brother-and-sister

Several people work to make a set look just right before the camera even starts to shoot.

detective team and their dog. They uncover a magical mansion. Madison has decided that she wants to make the film. She has secured $10 million to make her movie. After months of scheduling and budgeting, it is time to begin production.

Auditions have been held and the actors have been working on their lines. It is the first day of shooting. The entire cast and crew are on location in Adirondack Park in upstate New York. Madison intends to shoot two scenes: one from the beginning of the movie, and the closing scene. The beginning is a nighttime campfire scene, which she wants to shoot before sunrise. The closing scene will be a daytime shot at the same location.

Each scene is divided into shoots. It is 4:00 A.M. and very dark outside. There is a lot of work to do.

Set designers and other experts have been on-site for days getting ready. They have set up tents and made a realistic campsite. Actors who play the detectives and their friends have been fitted for their costumes by wardrobe workers. An animal trainer is ready with Ralph, the dog who will play the detectives' pet. The lighting has been set up, and microphones are in place to capture the actors' lines.

"Quiet on the set!" yells Madison's assistant through her megaphone. The cameramen are ready. There are three cameras that will record the action from different perspectives.

"Lights!" The lighting crew switches on the big lights, which illuminate the camp scene. "Camera!" The cameramen and sound engineers begin recording. "Action!" shouts Madison. The actors begin to recite their lines. After three **takes**, Madison is satisfied with the first shots.

Movie directors have their actors do many takes. Actors recite their lines several different times. This allows them to

Markers keep track of shots and takes. Later, the director can go back and know when something was shot and for which scene.

say their lines in different ways. It also allows the director to shoot from different angles and to try different ways of lighting the scene.

LEARNING & INNOVATION SKILLS

Directors have many different shots to choose from when filming a scene. One example is an extreme close-up. This shot focuses on sections of an actor's face, such as the eyes or mouth. Another type of shot is an extreme wide shot. Extreme wide shots show a very large area at once. The viewer probably won't see sharp details.

Directors know that different types of shots help shape a film's story. That's why directors think hard about which shots to use. They try to come up with fresh and original ways to shoot a scene. How can different shots affect the way an audience reacts to a scene?

A big part of a director's job is to keep the actors and everyone else motivated and energized about the film. Sometimes all that's needed is a little bit of positive encouragement.

Soon Madison's crew takes a break for lunch. After makeup and wardrobe changes for some of the actors, it is time to shoot the closing scene of the movie. After a few hours, the day's work is done. It is now almost 8:00 P.M., and everyone is exhausted. They all need a good night's rest.

Director Sofia Coppola comes from a filmmaking family. Her father is director Francis Ford Coppola.

21ˢᵀ CENTURY CONTENT

Can you name five famous female directors? That might be difficult to do. In some ways, movie directing is still a man's world. Less than a handful of female directors have ever been nominated for an Academy Award in the Best Director category. And a woman has never won. Some argue that a film directed by a woman will not appeal to a large audience.

Through the years, however, women such as Penny Marshall and Sofia Coppola have proven that films by female directors can be successes. Both have made movies that earned money and received great reviews. In addition, organizations such as Women in Film & Television have branches around the world. They address issues that affect female directors and other women in the entertainment industry.

In the morning, they will fly to the West Coast. Most of the film will be shot at a studio in Hollywood, California. In a few days, Madison wants everyone to be at the studio at 5:00 A.M. for another full day of shooting. After that, some city scenes will be filmed on location in Toronto, Canada.

CHAPTER THREE
CUT AND PRINT!

The cast and crew of *The Mystery of the Magic Mansion* have been shooting scenes for many weeks. The last bits of the movie have been filmed, but there is still more work to do.

Special effects need to look natural and realistic. The illusion of flight can require computer-generated effects and a stunt double.

At this stage, the movie is in hundreds of different pieces. Now begins the **postproduction** work. With the help of an editor, Madison pieces together the scenes in an order that makes sense. Madison also wants to incorporate computer-generated **special effects** into the film.

Unfortunately, some scenes that the actors and crew worked very hard on will have to be left out. Otherwise, the final product would be too long. Madison decides to cut a scene in which the kid detectives meet the queen of England. She realizes that the scene doesn't work with the flow of the story.

Cutting scenes involves making some tough decisions. After all, a lot of effort goes into each scene. The actors work hard rehearsing their lines. Experts in wardrobe spend a lot of time planning costumes. A director must determine if a scene helps the story line or distracts the audience. It's not always an easy decision. But making those decisions about the overall product is part of being a good movie director.

Postproduction work takes several months. Nearly one year after Madison first agreed to turn Jay's screenplay into a movie, it is time for opening night. Madison dresses up in her nicest outfit and has a limousine drive her to the theater for the **premiere**.

At a movie premiere, reporters and fans line up to see the director, actors, and other people who helped make the film. The people who have worked so hard on the film walk down a red carpet that leads into the theater. The public will see the film for the first time.

LEARNING & INNOVATION SKILLS

Many movie directors take part in media interviews to **promote** their films. Interviews can be a great way to get people excited about seeing a movie. They also give the director a chance to reflect on his or her work.

Strong speaking and communication skills are important tools for directors. These skills help them answer a journalist's questions clearly. Many people would agree that the best interview a director can give is one that sparks interest in the project. What are some ways you can work on becoming a better speaker?

Madison takes her seat in the theater. The lights go down. The projector in the back of the theater starts to flicker. The audience claps politely. Ninety minutes later, the movie ends. The audience erupts in applause. Madison smiles. Her film is a huge success!

Director Steven Spielsberg and his wife pose for a picture as they arrive at the theater for the premiere of his movie Minority Report.

CHAPTER FOUR
BECOMING A MOVIE DIRECTOR

The success of a movie takes a lot of hard work from many dedicated people. Thanks to Madison's leadership and creativity, her movie became a hit. A successful director will

Start filming your own movies now. Becoming a movie director takes a lot of practice.

probably go on to even bigger projects. So how does someone become a movie director?

The road to becoming a director is not a smooth one. Success in the industry takes hard work and **perseverance**. Working in the movie business is a very rewarding career. But those rewards do not come easily. Competition is fierce. If you are determined, however, you can be successful.

LEARNING & INNOVATION SKILLS

If you are interested in becoming a director, think about studying acting. Why think about acting when you want to direct? Many directors have worked as actors. Mel Gibson, Barbra Streisand, Ron Howard, and Robert Redford are just a few examples of actors who have experience in front of and behind the camera. Acting experience gives directors firsthand knowledge of the acting process. This can help them relate to the actors in their films.

If you are interested in making movies, start small. Volunteer to operate audiovisual equipment for your teachers.

Write short stories and share them with your friends and family. Try writing a play or even a screenplay. Invite friends to act out the parts.

 LIFE & CAREER SKILLS

A great way to learn about directing movies is to watch them. Try to see a variety of movies. But don't just watch films. Study them. Watch new films and old films. Watch films from your country and films from around the world. Pay careful attention to how the director uses different camera angles to help tell a story. Is the pace of the movie fast or slow? Why is one scene more powerful than another? Studying films is just another step toward becoming a great director. Observing other people's work can also help you find out which skills you need to improve. Does watching a well-made movie inspire you to direct your own?

Does your family own a video camera? Ask if you can use it to make short films about everyday things. Film your pet going about its day. Film your dad cooking. As you get

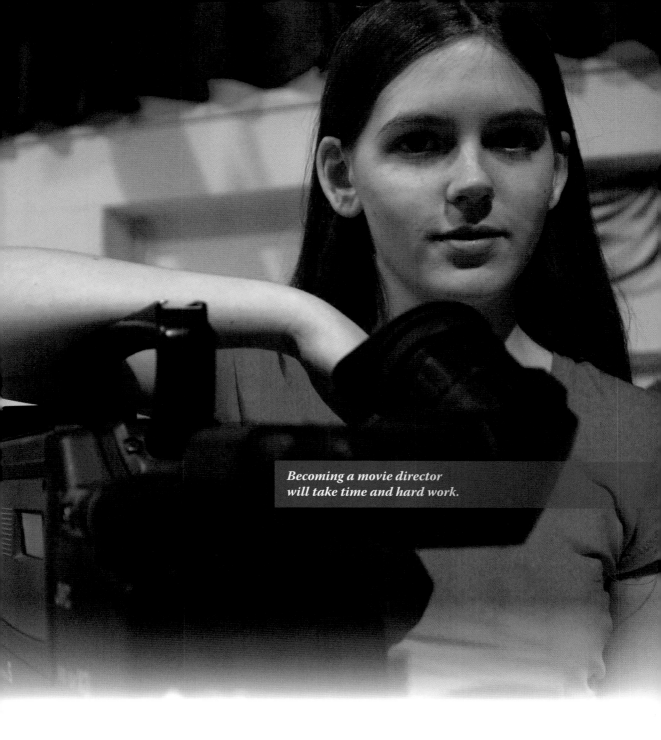

Becoming a movie director
will take time and hard work.

better at handling the camera, ask if you can operate it at family events. Little by little, you will become more comfortable using camera equipment. After you earn your parents' trust, maybe they will let you use the family camera to film one of your screenplays. You can even try making your own props and sets using items you find around the house. Or you can make props with simple art supplies.

Take some time to find out what resources are available. Your local library or school might show classic movies and have someone lead discussions about them. Maybe most important of all, write creatively and read as much as you can. Remember that directors are storytellers. Any director will tell you that his job would be impossible without good stories. Visit your school library, and read many kinds of stories. Never be afraid to read something new, even if you think you will not like it at first. Many famous movies are based on books.

If you are serious about becoming a movie director, you have a number of choices for formal education. Many universities have film departments where students can study the art of the motion picture. Film studies is a popular major with students who want to learn filmmaking and study the history of film. Some of the top film schools in the United States are New York University, the University of Southern California, and the University of California, Los Angeles.

Books and movies have a lot in common. Good storytelling is something that can be learned from both.

Students who major in film studies typically take courses on the history of American film, Asian film, and European film. They also study silent film and experimental film. Many film departments have classes on specific movie categories such as horror, science fiction, and animation. Knowing a lot about the history of film can help you develop your skills as a director.

Students who major in film also get to learn filmmaking techniques. Many universities have film studios where students can learn about film production. Students create their own films and learn how to edit them with computer software. At many of the best film schools, the teachers often have professional experience in the movie and television industries. You might learn screenwriting from someone who has written a famous screenplay. Or you might learn about sound editing from an award-winning editor.

College graduates can apply to study at the American Film Institute (AFI) Conservatory in Los Angeles, California. This famous program receives hundreds of applications each year, but only a small number of people are accepted. AFI students learn from some of the best film directors, editors, screenwriters, and actors in the business today.

You might not be old enough for college, but you do not have to wait to get some serious practice making films. With your parents' permission, you can even post homemade

Buster Keaton started making movies in 1917, and continued until 1966. His films may be old, but there is still a lot to learn from them.

videos on Web sites such as YouTube (www.youtube.com). Internet users have posted millions of videos on this site. What are you waiting for? Maybe a career in Hollywood is in your future!

Hollywood is not the only place movies are made. Many films are made in countries such as India and China.

SOME FAMOUS
MOVIE DIRECTORS

Sofia Coppola (1971–) is one of the world's leading female directors. Her film *Lost in Translation* won an Academy Award in 2004 for Best Original Screenplay. She is the daughter of famous director Francis Ford Coppola.

Spike Lee (1957–) is an African American director, actor, producer, and screenwriter. His films often explore controversial topics such as racial tensions. He is famous for many works, including the film *Malcolm X*. Lee is credited by many as being one of the first highly successful African American filmmakers.

Martin Scorsese (1942–) has directed nearly 50 films. He has also produced, written, and appeared in many films. He was honored by the American Film Institute with its Life Achievement Award in 1997. He has taught film classes at New York University. In addition to directing, Scorsese is also passionate about preserving old films and making them available to modern audiences.

Steven Spielberg (1946–) has directed a variety of successful films, including *Schindler's List* and *Jurassic Park*. This writer, producer, and director is one of the most important artists in the movie industry. He is also one of the world's most recognizable filmmakers. In 1994, Spielberg and a group of executives formed DreamWorks film studio.

Orson Welles (1915–1985) was a talented stage actor and radio personality. His masterpiece, *Citizen Kane*, was released in 1941. Not only did Welles direct *Citizen Kane*, he also co-wrote, produced, and starred in it. The film is praised as one of the best motion pictures of all time. He went on to make many other films.

GLOSSARY

auditions (aw-DISH-uhnz) performances that test the capabilities of actors who want a part in a movie or play

budget (BUHJ-it) a plan of how money will be spent and earned

cast (KAST) the group of performers who act in a play or movie

cinematographer (sih-nuh-muh-TAH-gruh-fur) a specialist in the art of motion picture photography

editors (ED-uh-turz) people who put filmed scenes together and arrange them into an orderly store

perseverance (pur-suh-VEER-uhns) the quality of not giving up

perspective (pur-SPEK-tiv) the way something is seen from a certain point of view

postproduction (POHST-pruh-duhk-shuhn) the stage after filming has been completed in which the footage is prepared for public viewing

premiere (pri-MEER) the first official public showing of a movie or play

promote (pruh-MOTE) to make people aware of something

screenplay (SKREEN-play) the script containing the story line, the words the actors will say, directions on where the actors should move, and suggestions on how the action should be filmed

set designers (SET di-ZINE-urz) people who plan and build locations that will be used as scenes where actors perform

special effects (SPESH-uhl uh-FEKTS) visual or sound elements added to footage to create scenes that can't be shot using ordinary filming techniques

takes (TAYKS) scenes filmed without interruption or stopping the camera

FOR MORE INFORMATION

BOOKS

Dunkleberger, Amy. *So You Want to Be a Film or TV Director?* Berkeley Heights, NJ: Enslow Publishers, 2008.

Edge, Laura B. *Steven Spielberg: Director of Blockbuster Films.* Berkeley Heights, NJ: Enslow Publishers, 2008.

Horn, Geoffrey M. *Writing, Producing, and Directing Movies.* Milwaukee, WI: Gareth Stevens Publishing, 2007.

WEB SITES

AFI.com: History of AFI
www.afi.com/about/history.aspx
Learn about the history of the American Film Institute

Bureau of Labor Statistics: Actors, Producers, and Directors
www.bls.gov/oco/ocos093.htm
Read more about a career as a movie director

Kids' Vid
kidsvid.altec.org/index.html
Find tips and information about writing scripts, filmmaking, and editing

Ultrabug Cliposcope
nfbkids.ca/ultrabug/web_en/
Make your own movies online at this National Film Board of Canada site

INDEX

ABOUT THE AUTHOR

Joseph R. O'Neill is a teacher, writer, and editor living in Hollywood, California—the heart of the motion picture industry. He has worked as an on-set consultant for a major motion picture studio and for television. He has also written several books for young people on topics ranging from the Great Wall of China to ancient Greek religion. Although he hasn't directed any movies, he sure does like to watch them.